WHAT THE BIBLE Actually Teaches

• • • • •

A | Workbook Designed to Teach and Establish Sound Doctrine in the Life of Every Believer.

Bill Scheidler

WHAT THE BIBLE Actually Teaches

. . . . .

Bill Scheidler

Unless otherwise noted, all Scripture references are taken from the New King James Version.
Copyright © 1984
Thomas Nelson, Inc.

What the Bible Actually Teaches
Copyright © 1992 Bible Temple

Available from:

BIBLE TEMPLE PUBLISHING
7545 N.E. Glisan Street
Portland, Oregon 97213-6396
(503) 253-9020

ISBN: 0-914936-78-6

All rights reserved. No portion of this book may be reproduced, stored in a retrieval system, or transmitted in any form or by any means electronic, mechanical, photocopy, recording, or any other except for brief quotations in printed reviews without the prior permission of the Publisher.

Printed in the United States of America

AUTHOR'S PREFACE

The Bible clearly instructs leaders to give themselves to doctrine so that they can exhort, convince and labor effectively in word and doctrine (I Timothy 4:13,16; 5:17; Titus 1:9).

Unfortunately, we are living in a day when very few believers know what the Bible actually teaches. Because of this, their "sword of the Spirit" is dull and they can easily become a target for seducing spirits and any other winds of doctrine that blow through the land (Ephesians 4:14; I Timothy 4:1).

The challenge in these days is to be nourished on the truth so that the false can be readily identified. The challenge of these days is to build on the strong foundation of sound doctrine so that we can truly build on the rock and endure the winds and storms that come.

The purpose of *What the Bible Actually Teaches* is to assist pastors and leaders in establishing sound doctrine in their churches and is an excellent book for self-study, devotional use, group or classroom setting, Bible study or as a follow-up for new Christians. Each lesson is designed to be a one hour teaching class or study & devotional time. Blanks have been included in each lesson to encourage more active student participation. However, all of the fill-ins for the blanks can be found on the answer sheets in the back of the book. The teacher may want to remove those pages in the Student Manual before distribution.

An excellent companion volume to this manual that would serve as a good teacher's guide for further information and fuller exposition is entitled <u>The Foundations of Christian Doctrine</u> by Kevin J. Conner, which is available from Bible Temple Publishing, 7545 N.E. Glisan Portland, Oregon 97213, (503) 253-9020.

I pray that as you use this manual you would be "rooted and built up in Him and established in the faith (Colossians 2:7)."

Bill
Scheidler

TABLE OF CONTENTS

OUTLINE OF TEXT ix
LESSON 1   WHY STUDY DOCTRINE? 1
LESSON 2   THE HOLY SCRIPTURES, PART I 7
LESSON 3   THE HOLY SCRIPTURES, PART II 11
LESSON 4   THE HOLY SCRIPTURES, PART III 15
LESSON 5   THE ONE TRUE GOD, PART I 21
LESSON 6   THE ONE TRUE GOD, PART II 25
LESSON 7   THE ONE TRUE GOD, PART III 31
LESSON 8   SATAN, PART I 35
LESSON 9   SATAN, PART II 41
LESSON 10   MAN, PART I 47
LESSON 11   MAN, PART II 51
LESSON 12   SIN, PART I 55
LESSON 13   SIN, PART II 61
LESSON 14   JESUS CHRIST, PART I 65
LESSON 15   JESUS CHRIST, PART II 69
LESSON 16   JESUS CHRIST, PART III 73
LESSON 17   JESUS CHRIST, PART IV 77
LESSON 18   ANGELS, PART I 81
LESSON 19   ANGELS, PART II 87
LESSON 20   THE HOLY SPIRIT, PART I 91
LESSON 21   THE HOLY SPIRIT, PART II 97
LESSON 22   THE HOLY SPIRIT, PART III 101
LESSON 23   THE CHURCH, PART I 105
LESSON 24   THE CHURCH, PART II 111
LESSON 25   THE CHURCH, PART III 117
LESSON 26   HEAVEN AND HELL 123
ANSWER KEY 129

OUTLINE OF TEXT

WHY STUDY DOCTRINE? 1
    What is doctrine? 1
    What is the basic goal of doctrinal study? .. 1
    Why is it important for us to study Bible
        doctrine? 1
    What are the requirements for doctrine? ... 4

THE HOLY SCRIPTURES, PART I 7
    What are the various <u>names and titles</u> given
        to the Bible, the Word of God? 7
    What does the Bible say concerning
        itself? 8
    Why is the Bible necessary? 9

THE HOLY SCRIPTURES, PART II 11
    What are some symbols connected with
        the Word of God and what do they
        tell us? 11

THE HOLY SCRIPTURES, PART III 15
    What do we mean by "plenary, verbal
        inspiration"? 15
    What is the difference between inspiration,
        illumination and revelation? 16
    What are some proofs for the inspiration of
        the Scripture? 17

THE ONE TRUE GOD, PART I 21
    What should be our attitude concerning
        the many different philosophies of
        man concerning the nature of God? 21
    What is wrong with trying to prove the
        existence of God? 21

How can finite man know the nature and person of an infinite God? 22
What are some of the Scriptural definitions of God which declare His nature and person? 22

THE ONE TRUE GOD, PART II 25
What does the Bible tell us about the nature of God? 25

THE ONE TRUE GOD, PART III 31
What does the Bible tell us about God's being? 31
How are the three persons of the Godhead designated in the Bible? 33

SATAN, PART I 35
What was Satan's original state? 35
How did Satan fall from this original state? 37
What were the results of Satan's sin? 38

SATAN, PART II 41
What is the present work and activity of Satan? 41
Does the believer need to fear Satan? ... 43
What judgement is awaiting Satan and his angels? 45

MAN, PART I 47
How was man created from the hand of God? 47
How did man fall from this original state? . 48
What were the effects of the fall? 50

MAN, PART II 51

What is the condition of every man that is
   born into the world? 51
What happens to man in redemption? ... 52
What happens after the new birth? 53

SIN, PART I 55
   What to we mean by the term "sin"? 55
   Where did sin originate? 58

SIN, PART II 61
   What is the extent of sin? 61
   What is the penalty for sin? Is it too
     severe? 62
   What is the root of sin? 63
   What is the remedy for sin? 63

JESUS CHRIST, PART I 65
   What do we mean when we say that
     Jesus Christ has two natures? 65

JESUS CHRIST, PART II 69
   Why was it necessary for the Word to
     become flesh? 69
   How does Jesus Christ fulfill the
     qualifications for a Redeemer? 70
   Why did Jesus Christ have to die? 70

JESUS CHRIST, PART III 73
   What was the death of Christ for man? ... 73
   What are the benefits of the atonement? . 75

JESUS CHRIST, PART IV 77
   What happened to Christ after His death? 77
   What is Christ doing now? 78
   What does the Bible teach concerning
     Christ's coming again? 79

ANGELS, PART I 81
   What is an angel? 81
   How do we know that angels exist? 81
   Why is the existence of angels questioned
      by some? 82
   What names and titles are ascribed to
      angels in the Bible? 83
   What is the nature of angels? 83

ANGELS, PART II 87
   What are some other things that we know
      about angels? 87
   What is the ministry and function of
      the angels? 88
   What specific area of God's dealing with
      man has **not** been
      entrusted to angels? 90

THE HOLY SPIRIT, PART I 91
   Is the Holy Spirit part of the Godhead? ... 91
   Is the Holy Spirit a person or merely a
      heavenly influence? 93
   How important is the Holy Spirit in our
      lives? 95

THE HOLY SPIRIT, PART II 97
   What are some of the names and titles
      ascribed to the Holy Spirit? 97
   What are some of the most common
      symbols that are applied to the
      Holy Spirit? 98

THE HOLY SPIRIT, PART III 101
   What is the work and ministry of the
      Holy Spirit? 101
   Why is it so important to know the Holy
      Spirit? 104

THE CHURCH, PART I	105
Why is it so important to study the doctrine of the Church?	105
What does the word "church" mean? ...	106
What did Jesus teach concerning the Church?	107
What aspect of the Church becomes the major focus of the New Testament?	109
THE CHURCH, PART II	111
What are some of the names and titles of the church?	111
What is the relationship of the Church in the Old Testament and the Church in the New Testament? ..	112
THE CHURCH, PART III	117
What does the book of Ephesians reveal to us about the Church?	117
What is the ministry and mission of the Church?	120
HEAVEN AND HELL	123
What happens to people when they die?	123
Is there a judgement after death?	124
What is heaven going to be like?	125
Is there a literal hell?	126
What will hell be like?	127
What makes our life on earth and the decisions that we make so important?	128

The Biblical Teaching Concerning
WHY STUDY DOCTRINE?

Colossians 2:7 "Rooted and built up in him and established in the faith, as you have been taught, abounding in it with thanksgiving."

LESSON ONE

I. **What is doctrine?**

   A. The word "doctrine" simply means "teaching" or "instruction."

   B. A Bible doctrine consists of __All That the Bible__ has to say on a particular subject.

II. **What is the basic goal of doctrinal study?**

   A. To give us an orderly understanding of basic biblical truths (Luke 1:1,4).

   B. To ground our faith solidly upon the Word of Truth (Colossians 2:7-8).

III. **Why is it important for us to study Bible doctrine?**

   A. Because it was important to __Jesus__. (John 17:8; Matthew 7:28-29; John 7:16).

WHAT THE BIBLE ACTUALLY TEACHES

B. Because it was important to **THE DISCIPLES**. (Luke 1:1-4).

C. Because it was important to **PAUL**. (I Timothy 6:1-3).

D. Because **THE EARLY CHURCH** saw it as one of the necessary essentials of body life (Acts 2:42).

E. Because it is God's means of progressing our development in Christian character (Isaiah 28:9-10; James 1:22-25).

   1. Right teaching leads to **RIGHTEOUS LIVING**. (Isaiah 2:3; Colossians 1:9-10).

   2. Right teaching leads to **CHRISTIAN FREEDOM**. (John 8:32,36).

   3. Right teaching leads to **SANCTIFICATION** (John 17:17; II Timothy 3:14-17; Ephesians 5:26).

   4. Right teaching leads to **MATURITY** (Colossians 1:27-28; Ephesians 4:11-13).

   5. Right teaching leads to **LIFE**. (Proverbs 16:21-23).

Why Study Doctrine? 3

      6.   Right teaching is the rain that will cause our lives to bear fruit (Deuteronomy 32:2).

F.   Because the last days will be characterized <u>By Deception.</u> (II Timothy 3:1-5).

      1.   Right teaching will help us to be able to judge true doctrine (I Timothy 1:3).

      2.   Right teaching will keep us from going astray (Proverbs 5:23; 8:33).

      3.   Right teaching will keep us from being blown about (Ephesians 4:14).

      4.   Right teaching will help us to be rooted in Him (Colossians 2:7)

      5.   Right teaching will give us a confidence in spiritual warfare when the battle is raging (II Timothy 1:12-13).

G.   Because we are commanded to "instruct" all nations (Matthew 28:20).

      1.   Right teaching will help us to give an answer to those who ask (I Peter 3:15).

      2.   Right teaching will help us to convince those who contradict (Titus 1:9).

3. Right teaching will enable us to teach others (II Timothy 2:2; Hebrews 8:11).

H. Because right teaching will bring peace to God's people (II Chronicles 15:3-5).

I. Because it affects our fellowship (II Thessalonians 3:6,14; II John 9-10).

J. Because it determines our destiny (John 14:6).

K. Because it is true spiritual riches (Proverbs 8:8-11).

L. Because it is pursued by the wise (Proverbs 9:9; 4:1-13; 19:20).

1. Right teaching is hated by the wicked (Psalm 50:17).

2. Right teaching is despised by the fool (Proverbs 1:7).

M. Because God is restoring the teaching ministry to the Church that the Church might fully enter into the purposes of God (Isaiah 30:20; Ephesians 4:8-13).

IV. What are the requirements for doctrine?

A. Doctrine must be _Sound_
(I Timothy 1:10; II Timothy 4;3; Titus 2:1).

B. Doctrine must be __PURE__ (Titus 2:7).

C. Doctrine must be based on __SCRIPTURE__ (II Timothy 3:14-17).

D. Doctrine must be __PRACTICED__ (Romans 6:17; Matthew 16:12 with 23:1-3).

Isaiah 29:24 "These also who erred in spirit will come to understanding, and those who complained will learn doctrine."

The Biblical Teaching Concerning
THE HOLY SCRIPTURES, PART I

II Timothy 3:16-17 "All Scripture is given by inspiration of God, and is profitable for doctrine, for reproof, for correction, for instruction in righteousness, that the man of God may be complete, thoroughly equipped for every good work."

LESSON TWO

I. What are the various <u>names and titles</u> given to the Bible, the Word of God?

    A. THE BIBLE: The word "Bible" comes from the Greek word *biblios* which simply means *book* (John 20:30; Hebrews 10:7; Revelation 22:7, 9-10, 18-19).

    B. THE HOLY BIBLE: Although this term is never found in the Bible itself, it is a good term, for it describes the nature of the Book of Books.

    C. THE SCRIPTURE: This word literally means *writings* and refers specifically to the written Word of God as opposed to that which is oral (Matthew 21:42; 22:29; 26:54).

    D. THE WORD OF GOD (or simply THE WORD): The Bible not only contains the Word of God, but it **is** the Word of God. It is God's Word to His creation. It is God's letter to man (Romans 10:17; Hebrews 4:12; I Thessalonians 2:13).

E. THE OLD AND NEW TESTAMENTS: The word *testament* means *will* or *covenant*. This book contains God's heritage or God's will to man (Exodus 24:7; II Corinthians 3:14).

F. THE ORACLES OF GOD: The word *oracle* means *speaking place*. God presently speaks to us through Jesus Christ His Son (Hebrews 1:1-2), but it is the Word of God that is the means through which He speaks. If we want to know what God says, we should consult the oracles of the Word of God (Romans 3:2).

II. **What does the Bible say concerning itself?**

A. The Bible claims to be _DIVINELY INSPIRED_ (II Timothy 3:16; Exodus 17:14).

B. The Bible claims to be _THE FINAL AUTHORITY_ and, hence, the final court of appeal and only source and norm for all doctrine (Deuteronomy 4:2; Revelation 22:18-19; Galatians 1:8-9).

C. The Bible demands _OBEDIENCE_. as only God can expect (Luke 24:25-27; John 8:31-32; 12:48).

III. Why is the Bible necessary?

> The Bible is absolutely necessary for man to have an intimate knowledge of God. If God would not reveal Himself to man, there would be no way in which man could know God!

    A. God has revealed Himself to man by primarily three avenues:

        1. God has revealed Himself to man in _CREATION_.

           (Romans 1:18-21; Psalm 19:1-6). Creation reveals God's power.

        2. God has revealed Himself to man through the _CONSCIENCE_ (Romans 2:14-16). Conscience reveals God as a moral being.

        3. God has revealed Himself to man by _DIVINE INTERVENTION_.

           (Hebrews 1:1-2; Numbers 7:89; II Samuel 23:2). The Word of God reveals God's nature and His plan for man.

    B. It is only by the means of the Scripture that we can know and experience salvation (II Timothy 3:15; Romans 10:17).

C. The Scriptures are able to give us a confident hope for the future (Romans 15:4).

The Biblical Teaching Concerning
THE HOLY SCRIPTURES, PART II

Hebrews 4:12 "For the word of God is living and powerful, and sharper than any two-edged sword, piercing even to the division of soul and spirit, and of joints and marrow, and is a discerner of the thoughts and intents of the heart."

LESSON THREE

IV. What are some symbols connected with the Word of God and what do they tell us?

    A. The Word of God is a _HAMMER_. (Jeremiah 23:29). It is able to break up and make an impression on hard hearts.

    B. The Word of God is a _MIRROR_. (II Corinthians 3:18; James 1:23-25). It reveals to man his true spiritual condition.

    C. The Word of God is a _TWO-EDGED SWORD_ (Ephesians 6:17; Hebrews 4:12). It works **for** us to bring victory to our lives. It works **on** us to convict and divide (II Timothy 3:16; James 1:23-24).

12 WHAT THE BIBLE ACTUALLY TEACHES

D. The Word of God is a __JUDGE__.
(Hebrews 4:12 In the Greek the word "discerner" literally means a critic or judge). The Word of God passes right judgment on the innermost nature of man.

E. The Word of God is __WATER__.
(John 15:3; Ephesians 5:26). It cleanses and purifies the soul from the defilement of sin (Psalm 119:9).

F. The Word of God is __SEED__.
(Luke 8:11; I Peter 1:23). It is sown in the heart to bring forth spiritual fruit.

G. The Word of God is __FOOD__.
(Jeremiah 15:16). It is that which imparts strength to the spiritual man (Deuteronomy 8:3; Psalm 119:103; Job 23:12; Jeremiah 15:16).

   1. It is **milk** for babes (I Peter 2:2; Hebrews 5:12-13).

   2. It is **bread** for the mature (Isaiah 55:1-2; Matthew 4:4).

   3. It is **strong meat** for the adult (I Corinthians 3:2; Hebrews 5:12-14).

   4. It is sweet and delightful as **honey** (Psalm 19:10).

The Holy Scriptures, Part II 13

H. The Word of God is a _LAMP_
(Psalm 119:105; Proverbs 6:23; II Peter 1:19).

  1. It imparts life to darkened man (John 6:63; II Corinthians 3:18).

  2. It exposes areas of sin in our lives (Hebrews 4:12-13).

  3. It gives direction and guidance (Proverbs 6:22-23).

I. The Word of God is _TRUE RICHES_
(Psalm 19:10; 119:72). It makes the possessor rich and wise.

J. The Word of God is a _FIRE_
(Jeremiah 20:9; 23:29).

  1. It warms the heart.

  2. It gives zeal for service.

  3. It exposes the wood, hay and stubble in our life (I Corinthians 3:12-15).

The Biblical Teaching Concerning
THE HOLY SCRIPTURES, PART III

II Peter 1:20-21 "Knowing this first, that no prophecy of Scripture is of any private interpretation, for prophecy never came by the will of man, but holy men of God spoke as they were moved by the Holy Spirit."

LESSON FOUR

V. What do we mean by "plenary, verbal inspiration"?

    A. The word *plenary* means _Full or Complete_.

    Plenary inspiration means that the entire Bible is totally inspired by God.

        1. Inspiration does not merely apply to portions of the Bible, but it applies to _The Entire Book_.

        2. Inspiration does not merely apply to doctrinal issues, but it applies to _Every Area_ _____ covered.

    B. The word *verbal* means *relating to words*.

WHAT THE BIBLE ACTUALLY TEACHES

1. Verbal inspiration means that God not only gave the subject matter to be recorded, but _THE VERY WORDS_ that are used are inspired of God (Jeremiah 1:9; I Thessalonians 2:13; I Chronicles 28:11-12,19).

2. Verbal inspiration does **not** mean that the writers were in a trance and that their personalities were totally overruled by the Spirit.

3. Verbal inspiration means that the Scripture is perfectly inerrant (_WITHOUT ERROR._) in all of its words and in _EVERY USE_ of its words (John 10:35b; Matthew 5:17-19; Acts 24:14).

C. The word *inspiration* means _GOD-BREATHED._ (II Timothy 3:16-17; II Peter 1:21).

VI. **What is the difference between inspiration, illumination and revelation?**

A. Revelation is the act _OF COMMUNICATING_ divine knowledge to man (Deuteronomy 29:29).

B. Illumination is the divine ability _TO UNDERSTAND_

that which is given by revelation (I Peter 1:10-12; Luke 24:32,45).

C. Inspiration of Scripture is the divine ability __ TO WRITE DOWN __ Revelation without making a mistake (II Peter 1:21).

VII. **What are some proofs for the inspiration of the Scripture?**

A. There are many internal proofs for inspiration.

1. The Bible claims to be inspired (II Timothy 3:15-16).

2. The phrase "thus saith the Lord" occurs over 2000 times.

3. The Old Testament portions which are referred to in the New Testament are referred to in such a way as to indicate inspiration (Matthew 1:22; Hebrews 3:7).

4. Christ and the apostles treated the Scripture as being inspired (Matthew 8:16-17).

5. There is great authority suggested in the phrase, "it is written" (Matthew 4:7; Luke 4:10; Galatians 3:10).

B. There are also many external proofs for the inspiration of the Scriptures.

1. One of the greatest proofs is the fact of fulfilled prophecy. Note a few of the Messianic prophecies that were fulfilled, in some cases over 500 years after they were uttered.

    a. Christ to be born in Bethlehem (Micah 5:2; Matthew 2:1-8).

    b. Christ to come after 483 years (Daniel 9:25; Mark 1:15).

    c. Christ sold for thirty pieces of silver (Zechariah 11:13; Matthew 26:14-15; 27:3-10).

    d. Christ crucified (Psalm 22; Isaiah 53).

    e. Christ's garments divided (Psalm 22:18; John 19:23; Matthew 27:35).

    f. Christ's burial with the rich (Isaiah 53:9; Matthew 27:57-60).

2. The miraculous spread of the Gospel is a proof of the truth of what is claimed.

3. The fact that no other religion in the world transforms men like Christianity attests to the validity and power of the Word of God.

4. The miraculous preservation of the Bible in spite of numerous attempts throughout history to destroy it attests to its validity.

5. The fact that the early apostles who would have known the truth or falsehood of the resurrection were willing to die rather than to forsake the truth attests to its validity. No one would be so willing to die for a lie.

The Biblical Teaching Concerning
THE ONE TRUE GOD, PART I

Hebrews 11:6 "But without faith it is impossible to please Him, for he who comes to God must believe that He is, and that He is a rewarder of those who diligently seek Him."

LESSON FIVE

I. **What should be our attitude concerning the many different philosophies of man concerning the nature of God?**

   A. We should avoid such things as unprofitable (Colossians 2:8).

   B. We should realize that natural man will never be able to understand the things of God (I Corinthians 2:11-14; Ecclesiastes 8:17).

   C. We should realize that natural man is likely to conceptualize God in such a way as to soothe his conscience (Micah 4:5; Psalm 106:20).

II. **What is wrong with trying to prove the existence of God?**

A. This usually ends up in an argument and confusion.

B. This is something that the Bible itself never does.

1. The Bible never attempts to prove the existence of God; it only _DECLARES IT_ (Genesis 1:1; John 1:1).

2. The Bible declares that this _KNOWLEDGE OF GOD_ is given to every man (Romans 1:19-21,28,32).

III. How can finite man know the nature and person of an infinite God?

A. The knowledge of God is foundational to any approach to God (Hebrews 11:6).

B. The knowledge of God is insufficient in itself to bring salvation (James 2:19).

C. The knowledge of the person and nature of God can only come to man as God reveals it to him (Matthew 11:27; Ephesians 4:17-21).

IV. What are some of the Scriptural definitions of God which declare His nature and person?

A. God is _SPIRIT_ (John 4:24).

B. God is _LIGHT_ (I John 1:5).

C. God is _LOVE_ (I John 4:8,16).

D. God is a _CONSUMING FIRE_. (Hebrews 12:29; Deuteronomy 4:24).

(NOTE TO TEACHER: If time remains, proceed to the next lesson and Question V.)

The Biblical Teaching Concerning
THE ONE TRUE GOD, PART II

Exodus 15:11 "Who is like You, O Lord, among the gods? Who is like You, glorious in holiness, fearful in praises, doing wonders?"

LESSON SIX

V. **What does the Bible tell us about the nature of God?**

    A. There are certain natural attributes or qualities that belong to God.

        1. God is **eternal**, that is, He has no beginning and no end (Genesis 21:33; Psalm 90:2; 102:24; Isaiah 40:28; 44:6; Habakkuk 1:12; Revelation 11:17).

        2. God is **immutable**, that is, He never changes (Numbers 23:19; I Samuel 15:29; Malachi 3:6; Hebrews 6:17-18; James 1:17).

        3. God is **independent**, that is, He is totally self-sufficient (John 1:1-3).

            a. God depends on **no one** for His existence (Psalm 36:9; John 5:26).

- b. God depends on **no one** for His knowledge (Hebrews 4:13; Isaiah 40:12-14).

- c. God depends on **no one** for His actions (Genesis 1:1; Acts 17:24-28).

- d. God depends on **no one** for His supply (I Timothy 6:15-16; Acts 17:25).

4. God is **omnipotent,** that is, He has power over _EVERYTHING_. (Genesis 18:14; Jeremiah 32:27).

    - a. God has power over nature (Psalm 33:6-9; Nahum 1:3-6).

    - b. God has power over man (James 4:12-15; Exodus 4:11).

    - c. God has power over all angels (Daniel 4:35).

    - d. God has power over Satan (Job 1:12; 2:6).

    - e. God has power over death (Ephesians 1:19-21; I Corinthians 15:24-26).

5. God is **omniscient**, that is, He knows <u>EVERYTHING.</u>
(Romans 11:33; I John 3:20).
(Much in this section comes from <u>What the Bible Teaches</u> by R.A. Torrey)

   a. He sees all that occurs in every place and keeps watch upon the evil and the good (Proverbs 15:3).

   b. He knows everything that occurs in nature (Psalm 147:4; Matthew 10:29; 6:8).

   c. He knows the ways of man (Psalm 33:13-15; Proverbs 5:21).

   d. He knows all man's deeds and experiences (Psalm 139:2-3).

   e. He knows all man's words (Psalm 139:4).

   f. He knows all man's sorrows (Exodus 3:7).

   g. He knows all our thoughts (Psalm 139:1-2; I Chronicles 28:9).

   h. God knows for all eternity what will be for all eternity (Acts 15:18).

WHAT THE BIBLE ACTUALLY TEACHES

6. God is **omnisapient**, that is, He possesses all _WISDOM_. (Romans 11:33; 16:27; I Timothy 1:17).

7. God is **omnipresent**, that is, He is _EVERYWHERE_ in the universe at all times (Psalm 139:7-10; Jeremiah 23:23-24).

B. There are certain moral attributes or qualities that belong to God.

1. God is absolutely _HOLY_. (Psalm 22:3; 99:5,9; Isaiah 5:16; 6:3; Zephaniah 3:5; John 17:11; I Peter 1:15-16).

2. God is and has perfect _LOVE_. (Jeremiah 31:3; John 3:16; I John 4:8,16; Romans 5:8; 8:39).

3. God is absolutely _FAITHFUL_. (I Corinthians 1:9; 10:13; I Thessalonians 5:24; Deuteronomy 7:7-9).

4. God is absolutely _RIGHTEOUS or JUST_. (Ezekiel 18:19-30; Ezra 9:15; Psalm 116:5; 145:17; John 17:25; Revelation 15:3).

5. God is full of _MERCY_. (Psalm 103:8; Deuteronomy 4:31; Psalm 145:8-9).

Deuteronomy 32:4 "He is the rock, His work is perfect; for all His ways are justice, a God of truth and without injustice; righteous and upright is He."

The Biblical Teaching Concerning
THE ONE TRUE GOD, PART III

Romans 1:20 "For since the creation of the world His invisible attributes are clearly seen, being understood by the things that are made, even His eternal power and Godhead, so that they are without excuse."

LESSON SEVEN

VI. What does the Bible tell us about God's being?

    A. God is _ONE_. There is one God. He is the one and only God (Deuteronomy 4:35; 6:4; II Samuel 7:22; Isaiah 43:10; 44:6; 45:5,14,18; I Timothy 2:5; Mark 10:18; 12:29; Ephesians 4:6).

    B. God has _PLURALITY_ of being. This is seen in several ways.

        1. It is seen in the plural name "Elohim" (Genesis 1:1).

        2. It is seen in the use of plural pronouns in relation to God (Genesis 1:26; 3:22; 11:7).

        3. It is seen in other scriptural designations (Isaiah 48:16; 61:1; 63:8-10; Genesis 18:1-2,33).

WHAT THE BIBLE ACTUALLY TEACHES

C. God is a _TRI-UNITY_ (I John 5:7-8).

1. This is affirmed by the triple expressions ascribed to God (Isaiah 6:3; Numbers 6:24-26; Revelation 4:8; Matthew 28:19-20; II Corinthians 13:14).

2. This is exemplified in man who is made in the image of God (Genesis 1:26; I Thessalonians 5:23).

   a. As God is one, so man is one.

   b. As God is a tri-unity, so man is a tri-unity (spirit, soul and body).

   c. As with God two parts are invisible and one part is visible, so it is with man (spirit and soul).

3. This is portrayed in Bible types.

   a. The Tabernacle of Moses was a tri-une structure (outer court, holy place, most holy place, Exodus 26-27).

   b. The Lid of the Mercy Seat was a tri-une structure (cherubim, mercy seat, cherubim, Exodus 25:19).

   c. Aaron's rod had a tri-une manifestation of fruitfulness (buds, blossoms, almond fruit, Numbers 17:8).

    d. Noah's ark was a tri-une structure (Genesis 6:16).

4. It is revealed by God in a three part name (Exodus 3:15).

5. It is revealed by the natural things of creation (Romans 1:20).

    a. The heavenly bodies (sun, moon, stars) speak of God's tri-unity.

    b. The primary colors in nature (yellow, red, blue) speak of God's tri-unity.

VII. How are the three persons of the Godhead designated in the Bible?

There are three persons in the Godhead, namely, the FATHER, the SON, and the HOLY SPIRIT.

A. These are all recognized as God.

    1. The Father is _God_ (Romans 1:7; John 6:27; I Peter 1:2).

    2. The Son is _God_ (Hebrews 1:8; Titus 2:13-14; John 1:1,14).

    3. The Holy Spirit is _God_ (Acts 5:3-4).

B. There is a recognized order of headship in the Godhead but also equality of person (I Corinthians 11:3; Matthew 28:19; Philippians 2:6).

C. These three persons are distinguished in the Scriptures (Luke 3:21-22; John 14:16,26; 15:26; 16:7,10,13-15; Acts 2:33; 7:55-56; Ephesians 2:18; Acts 10:38; Ephesians 3:14-16; Philippians 3:3; Hebrews 9:14; I Peter 1:2; 3:18; Jude 20-21; Revelation 1:4-5).

DOCTRINAL STATEMENT

We believe in the eternal Godhead who has revealed Himself as one God existing in three persons: the Father, the Son, and the Holy Spirit; distinguishable but indivisible.

The Biblical Teaching Concerning SATAN, PART I

I John 3:8 "He who sins is of the devil, for the devil has sinned from the beginning. For this purpose the Son of God was manifested, that He might destroy the works of the devil."

LESSON EIGHT

I. **What was Satan's original state?**

   A. Satan was part of God's creation (Ezekiel 28:15; Colossians 1:16).

      1. As a created being he is much _INFERIOR TO GOD_.

      2. As a created being he is _FINITE_, hence not omniscient, omnipotent, omnipresent or self-existent.

   B. Satan is a spirit being of the _ANGELIC ORDER_.
(Isaiah 14:12-13; Matthew 25:41; II Corinthians 11:14; Revelation 12:9).

      1. He is, therefore, invisible, though as an angel he may manifest himself in temporary visible form.

2. He seems to be of the order of cherubim (Ezekiel 28:14,16).

C. Satan appears to have been the __*HIGHEST RANK*__ among the angelic orders.

1. Satan was full of wisdom (Ezekiel 28:12).

2. Satan was perfect in beauty (Ezekiel 28:12).

3. Satan was in Eden, the garden of God (Ezekiel 28:13). This was probably not the Eden of Genesis 1-2, but most likely refers in earthly terms to God's paradise in heaven.

4. Satan was covered with precious stones (Ezekiel 28:13; compare Exodus 28:15ff).

5. Satan had music within himself (Ezekiel 28:13).

   a. Cherubim seem to have a ministry in leading worship (Revelation 4:9-10).

   b. Satan was perhaps the worship leader of the universe. "If so, he tried to direct to himself what properly belonged to God" (Torrey).

6. Satan was the anointed cherub which perhaps distinguished him from others (Ezekiel 28:14).

7. Satan had a covering ministry in relation to the throne (Ezekiel 28:14; compare Exodus 37:9).

8. Satan was upon the holy mountain of God (Ezekiel 28:14), most likely the place of the visible manifestation of His glory (Psalm 48:1; Isaiah 2:3).

9. Satan walked up and down in the midst of the stones of fire (Ezekiel 28:14).

10. Satan was perfect in all his ways (Ezekiel 28:12,15).

11. Satan was very high in his authority, even over archangels (Jude 8-9).

12. Satan had a very large kingdom (Ephesians 2:2; 6:12).

13. Satan was a free moral agent, capable of choosing good or evil.

II. How did Satan fall from this original state?

A. Satan desired to claim for himself (worship) that which he was to direct to God alone (Isaiah 14:12-13; see notes on "Sin" II, A, page 61 of this manual).

1. His heart was lifted up within him because of his beauty (Ezekiel 28:17).

2. Iniquity was found within him (Ezekiel 28:15,17).

B. Satan led a conspiracy by soliciting other angels to follow after his cause (Ezekiel 28:16,18; Matthew 25:41; Revelation 12:4,9).

III. What were the results of Satan's sin?

A. Satan was cast forth from the heaven of heavens (Isaiah 14:12; Ezekiel 28:16-17).

B. Satan lost his state of perfection and became the _AUTHOR OF SIN_.
(Ezekiel 28:17; I John 3:8,10; John 8:44; Acts 13:10).

C. Satan perverted his power and abilities in use _AGAINST GOD_.
(Ezekiel 28:12,16-17).

D. Satan became the enemy of _GOD'S PURPOSES_.
(Ephesians 6:11-12; I Peter 5:8; Revelation 12:10).

E. Satan forfeited his previous kingdom, but gained for himself another.

1. He became the ruler of the fallen angels (Matthew 12:24-28; 25:41; Revelation 12:9).

2. He became the ruler of the world system (John 12:31; 16:11). This includes all the fallen angels and all those who are separated by sin from God's presence.

3. He became the god of this age (II Corinthians 4:4; Galatians 1:4).

The Biblical Teaching Concerning SATAN, PART II

I Peter 5:8 "Be sober, be vigilant; because your adversary the devil walks about like a roaring lion, seeking whom he may devour."

LESSON NINE

IV. **What is the present work and activity of Satan?** (The following outline taken from *Angels* by Dickason)

    A.   Satan opposes God.

           1.   He opposes God's person (I John 3:7-15).

           2.   He opposes all God's plans and purposes.

                  a.   He puts forth a lie (Ephesians 2:2; II Thessalonians 2:8-12).

                  b.   He inspires counterfeit religions (II Corinthians 11:13-15).

                  c.   He promotes false doctrine (I Timothy 4:1-3).

3. He counteracts God's sovereign rule (Matthew 4:1-11; John 13:26-30).

B. Satan works in relation to the nations.

1. He deceives nations (Revelation 20:3).

2. He influences the governments of nations (Matthew 4:8-10; Daniel 10:13-20).

C. Satan works in relation to the unsaved.

1. He tries to prevent them from accepting the truth (Luke 8:12; II Corinthians 4:3-4).

2. He promotes an attraction to false religions and false lifestyles (I Timothy 4:1-3; Ephesians 2:1-3; I John 2:15-17).

D. Satan works in relation to believers.

1. He wages warfare against them (Ephesians 6:10-18).

2. He accuses and slanders them before God (Revelation 12:10).

3. He plants doubts in their minds (Genesis 3:1-5).

4. He tempts them to sin (Acts 5:3; I Corinthians 7:5).

5. He incites persecution against them (Revelation 2:10; 12:13).

6. He tries to hinder their service to the Lord (I Thessalonians 2:18).

7. He tries to infiltrate the church through false teachers (II Corinthians 11:13-15; II Peter 2:1-19) and false disciples (Matthew 13:38-39).

8. He promotes division (II Corinthians 2:10-11).

9. He tries to afflict us physically (Luke 13:16).

V. **Does the believer need to fear Satan?**

YES AND NO!

A. The believer needs to recognize that Satan is a _POWERFUL_ enemy and not to be taken lightly.

1. We should be sober and watchful (I Peter 5:8).

2. We should not be ignorant of his devices (II Corinthians 2:11).

3. We should give him no place (Ephesians 4:27).

44   WHAT THE BIBLE ACTUALLY TEACHES

    4. We should resist him (James 4:7; I Peter 5:9; I John 2:13).

B. The believer needs to realize that in Christ we have been given _THE VICTORY_ over every work of the enemy (Colossians 2:14-16).

Correspond these points with those in Section IV, D and see that:

1. He has given us divine _ARMOUR + WEAPONS_ with which to fight and overcome Satan (Ephesians 6:11-18; II Corinthians 10:3-5).

2. He Himself _INTERCEDES_ in our behalf (I John 2:1-2).

3. He has given us _CONFIDENCE_ and faith (II Timothy 1:12; Philippians 1:6).

4. He has given us the _POWER_ to cast down evil imaginations (II Corinthians 10:3-5).

5. He uses the persecution of Satan to _INCREASE_ the church (Acts 8:1-4).

6. He sends us a Comforter to stand _ALONG SIDE US_. (John 14:16-18).

7. He has given us _DIVINE TESTS_ by which to judge error (Matthew 7:16; I John 2:14; 4:1-3).

8. He has given us all the elements to achieve perfect _UNITY_. (Ephesians 4:1-16).

9. He has taken our _SICKNESS_ upon Himself (Matthew 8:16-17).

10. He has given us the _LEGAL RIGHT_ to use His name (Mark 16:17-18; Acts 16:18).

VI. **What judgement is awaiting Satan and his angels?**

A. Satan was bruised judicially at the cross (Genesis 3:15; Colossians 2:14-16).

B. Satan is still walking about deceiving (I Peter 5:8).

C. Satan will be further bruised under the feet of the Church (Romans 16:20; Ephesians 1:21-23; I Corinthians 15:25-26).

D. Satan will ultimately be cast into the lake of fire with all his angels and demonic hosts (Matthew 25:41; Revelation 20:10-15).

The Biblical Teaching Concerning MAN, PART I

Genesis 1:26 "Then God said, Let Us make man in Our image, according to Our likeness; let them have dominion over the fish of the sea, over the birds of the air, and over the cattle, over all the earth and over every creeping thing that creeps on the earth."

LESSON TEN

I. **How was man created from the hand of God?**

   A. Man was created in the image of God (Genesis 1:26).

   1. This image involves man _AS A THREE-FOLD BEING._ (I Thessalonians 5:23).

      a. Man has a **spirit** (Zechariah 12:1; Job 32:8). This is the _GOD-CONSCIOUS_ part of man.

      b. Man has a **soul** (Ezekiel 18:4; Psalm 16:10; 19:7). This is the _SELF-CONSCIOUS_ part of man.

WHAT THE BIBLE ACTUALLY TEACHES

      c. Man has a **body** (Romans 12:1; Philippians 3:21). This is the <u>SENSE - CONSCIOUS</u> part of man.

  2. This image involves man <u>AS A INTELLIGENT BEING.</u> (Colossians 3:10).

  3. This image involves man <u>AS A MORAL BEING</u> (Ephesians 4:23-24).

B. Man was created <u>AS A DEPENDENT BEING.</u> (Acts 17:24-28).

C. Man was created to <u>BE INHABITED.</u> (John 14:17; I Corinthians 3:16-17).

D. Man was created for <u>LOVE.</u> (I John 4:16-19).

II. How did man fall from this original state?

A. Satan undermined the Word of God.

  1. Satan placed a question mark on God's word trying to get Eve to doubt when he said, "Has God indeed said?" (Genesis 3:1; II Corinthians 11:2-3).

Man, Part I 49

2. Satan contradicted the Word of God forcing Eve to make a choice when he said, "You will not surely die." (Genesis 3:4).

3. Satan cast doubt on God's intention and character in His dealings with man (Genesis 3:5). He implied that God was selfish and withholding something that was good for them.

4. Satan deceived them by only telling what they would gain, not what they would lose (cost) in the process (Genesis 3:5).

B. Man was tempted in the three areas of his being (I John 2:16).

1. He was tempted in the area of the _Body_, the lust of the flesh. He saw that it was good for food (Genesis 3:6).

2. He was tempted in the area of the _Soul_, the lust of the eyes. The eyes are the window of the soul (Genesis 3:6).

3. He was tempted in the area of the _Spirit_, the pride of life. He wanted to be wise and be like God (Genesis 3:6).

C. Man knowingly transgressed the law (I John 3:4).

III. What were the effects of the fall?

A. The conscience of man was activated (Genesis 3:7).

B. Man recognized the need for a covering (Genesis 3:7).

C. Man was cut off from fellowship with God (Genesis 3:8).

D. Man became fearful of God's presence (Genesis 3:8).

E. Death passed upon all men (Romans 5:12,19).

F. Man's spirit and mind were darkened (Proverbs 20:27; Ephesians 4:18).

The Biblical Teaching Concerning MAN, PART II

II Corinthians 3:18 "But we all, with unveiled face, beholding as in a mirror the glory of the Lord, are being transformed into the same image from glory to glory, just as by the Spirit of the Lord."

LESSON ELEVEN

IV. **What is the condition of every man that is born into the world?**

    A. Man is _Born_ in sin and, hence, is a sinner (Psalm 51:5; Romans 3:9-10, 22-23; Psalm 14:2-3; Isaiah 53:6; I John 1:8,10).

    B. Man has absolutely _No Inclination_ toward God (Romans 7:17-20; John 3:19; Jeremiah 17:9; Genesis 3:8).

    C. Man has absolutely _No Understanding_ of the things of God (I Corinthians 2:14).

    D. Man's mind is _Defiled_ by sin and separation (Titus 1:15; Colossians 1:21; Romans 8:7).

    E. Man is a _Slave_ to sin (Romans 6:17; 7:5,8,14-15,19,23-24).

WHAT THE BIBLE ACTUALLY TEACHES

- F. Man is a child of __WRATH__ (Ephesians 2:3).

- G. Man is an __ENEMY__ of God (Romans 8:7-8).

- H. Man is __DEAD__ in trespasses and sins (Ephesians 2:1).

- I. Man is on the road to eternal __DAMNATION__. (II Thessalonians 1:8-9; John 15:6).

V. **What happens to man in redemption?**
(The following is taken from unpublished notes by Kevin J. Conner.)

- A. There is an impartation of life to the human spirit (Psalm 18:28; John 1:4-14; 8:12; Ephesians 5:8; I Thessalonians 5:4-5; I Peter 2:9).

- B. There is a regeneration of our old spirit which was in darkness (John 3:1-5; Ezekiel 36:25-28; Titus 3:5; I Peter 1:23; Colossians 3:10).

- C. When we receive Christ as Savior, He puts His Spirit with our spirit and our spirit becomes one with the Holy Spirit (I Corinthians 6:17; John 1:12; Romans 8:9).

- D. We receive the evidence that this has taken place by the inward witness of the Spirit with our spirit (Galatians 4:6; Romans 8:15-16; I John 5:10).

VI. What happens after the new birth?
(The following is taken from unpublished notes by Kevin J. Conner.)

A. Our spirit still has a bent toward evil so the Spirit works continually, cleansing and renewing (II Corinthians 7:1).

B. The spirit of man is restored to a place of control over man. It should be noted that, although the spirit has dominion, there are many Christians who choose to obey the soul and the flesh. Hence we find three types of individuals:

1. The Natural Man: This is the unregenerate man outside of Christ (I Corinthians 2:14).

2. The Carnal Believer: This is the regenerate man who chooses to follow the animal instincts and the lusts of the flesh (I Corinthians 3:1-3).

3. The Spiritual Man: This is the regenerate man who is ruled by the Holy Spirit through his spirit (Romans 8:1-17).

C. As we yield to the Spirit, that Spirit which is in us begins to work in relation to the rest of this three-part being.

1. He breaks through the will of man.

2. He renews the conscience and mind of man.

3. His influence will one day sanctify the whole body (I Thessalonians 5:23).

D. Man will ultimately be restored to the image of God (Romans 8:29; II Corinthians 3:18).

The Biblical Teaching Concerning SIN, PART I

Romans 5:12,14 "Therefore, just as through one man sin entered the world, and death through sin, and thus death spread to all men, because all sinned ... Nevertheless death reigned from Adam to Moses, even over those who had not sinned according to the likeness of the transgression of Adam, who is a type of Him who was to come."

LESSON TWELVE

I. **What do we mean by the term "sin"?**

    A. First, it is important to understand what sin is not.

        1. Sin is not <u>AN ACCIDENT</u> (Romans 5:19).

        2. Sin is not <u>WEAKNESSES OF THE FLESH</u> (Hebrews 4:15).

        3. Sin is not <u>VARIOUS WORLD CALAMITIES</u> (e.g. floods, earthquakes, famines, etc.).

        4. Sin is not <u>A NECESSITY</u> for the believer (Romans 6:1-23).

56 WHAT THE BIBLE ACTUALLY TEACHES

5. Sin is not _Excusable_ (Ezekiel 18:4,20).

   a. Man would like to call it indiscretion.

   b. Scholars would like to label it ignorance.

   c. Others would like to call it moral weakness.

B. Second, it is important to see what the various words for sin mean in the Bible. The following are the English equivalents of the original Greek and Hebrew.

   1. *To miss the mark* (Judges 20:16). This is the most common meaning in both the Old and the New Testaments (Genesis 4:7; Exodus 9:27; Leviticus 5:1; Numbers 6:11; Psalm 51:2,4; Proverbs 8:36; Isaiah 42:24; Hosea 4:7; Romans 3:23; 5:12).

   2. *To be bent, twisted or crooked* (Exodus 20:5; Leviticus 5:1; Psalm 32:5; Isaiah 5:18; 53:5-6).

   3. *To have the habit of evil* (Job 16:11; 20:29; 34:8; Psalm 82:2; Proverbs 16:12; Isaiah 57:20-21; Malachi 2:6).

   4. *To rebel against authority* (Psalm 51:3; Proverbs 28:2; Isaiah 1:2; II Thessalonians 2:4,8).

5. *To cross over or go beyond a line, to transgress* (Psalm 17:3; Hosea 6:7; 8:1; Matthew 15:2-3; Romans 4:15).

6. *To wander from the path* (Ezekiel 34:6).

7. *To fall when one should have stood* (Galatians 6:1; Matthew 6:14; Ephesians 1:7; James 5:16).

8. *To neglect to hear or to disobey* (Matthew 18:17; Hebrews 2:2-3; Romans 5:19).

9. *To be ignorant of what should have been known* (Hebrews 9:7).

C. Third, it is important to see the various ways that the Bible defines sin.

1. Proverbs 21:4 - "An high look, and a proud heart, and the plowing of the wicked is sin."

2. Proverbs 24:9 - "The thought of foolishness is sin."

3. I John 3:4 - "Sin is transgression of the law."

4. I John 5:17 - "All unrighteousness is sin."

5. James 4:17 - "Knowing to do good and going it not is sin."

WHAT THE BIBLE ACTUALLY TEACHES

    6.   Romans 14:23 - "Whatsoever is not of faith is sin."

  D. Fourth, it is important to have a clear statement in regard to sin based on the biblical definitions.

> "Sin is any want of conformity unto, or transgression of, any law of God given as a rule to the reasonable creature."
> (The Large Catechism)

II. **Where did sin originate?**

  A. Sin entered the universe _THROUGH SATAN_.

    (Ezekiel 28:11-19; Isaiah 14:12-17).

    1. There was no sin prior to the transgression of Satan.

    2. Satan's sin was the sin of choosing his own will over God's will - the sin of **self-will** (Isaiah 14:13-14).

        a. **self**-ascendancy

        b. **self**-exaltation

        c. **self**-enthronement

Sin, Part I 59

   d. **self**-centeredness

   e. **self**-sufficiency

3. Satan's sin was the worst sin ever in that he sinned without a tempter.

B. Sin entered the human race _THROUGH ADAM_.
(Romans 5:19; Genesis 3:1-6; I Timothy 2:14).

The Biblical Teaching Concerning SIN, PART II

Romans 8:22-23 "For we know that the whole creation groans and labors with birth pangs together until now. Not only that, but we also who have the firstfruits of the Spirit, even we ourselves groan within ourselves, eagerly waiting for the adoption, the redemption of our body."

LESSON THIRTEEN

III. What is the extent of sin?

SIN HAS AFFECTED ALL THE CREATED UNIVERSE!

A. It has affected the _HEAVENLY PLACES_
(Hebrews 9:23; Ephesians 6:11-12).

B. It has affected the _NATURAL EARTH._
(Romans 8:22; Genesis 3:17-18).

C. It has affected the _ANIMAL KINGDOM._
(Genesis 9:2; Isaiah 11:6-9).

D. It has affected the _ENTIRE RACE OF MANKIND._

1. This fact is declared by the Scriptures (Romans 3:23; Galatians 3:22).

2. This fact is attested to by the people of the Lord (Job 40:4; Isaiah 6:5; Luke 5:8).

3. This fact is even testified to by the unsaved. Every man has a witness in his conscience of his own sinful condition.

   a. Seneca declared, "We have all sinned, some more and some less."

   b. Ovid wrote, "We all strive for what is forbidden."

   c. Goethe confessed, "I see no fault in others which I myself might not have committed."

   d. A Chinese proverb runs: "There are two good men: one is dead and the other is not yet born."

IV. What is the penalty for sin? Is it too severe?

   A. The ultimate penalty for all sin is eternal death (Genesis 2:17; Matthew 25:46; Romans 6:23; 5:12).

B. The worst aspect of the penalty is banishment from the presence of the Lord (II Thessalonians 1:7-9; Genesis 3:24; 4:16).

C. The penalty is just because:

1. Man's sin, no matter how great or small, reflects disloyalty and disobedience.

2. In man's sin, rebellion against God's authority over him was revealed.

3. Man sinned in full knowledge of the penalty to be incurred.

4. In man's sin, the condition of his heart was revealed: ambitious, ungrateful, rebellious and unbelieving.

V. What is the root of sin?

A. _Self Will._
(Isaiah 14:12-14).

B. _Pride._
(Proverbs 16:18).

C. _Covetousness._
(Romans 7:7; I Timothy 6:10).

D. _Unbelief._
(Hebrews 3:12,19; 4:6,11).

VI. What is the remedy for sin?

A. The only remedy for sin is the redemptive work of the Lord Jesus Christ (see "Jesus Christ", Part II and III, pages 69-76).

B. The only remedy for sin in man is to exercise faith (opposite of unbelief) in the redemptive work of Christ (Hebrews 11:6).

   1. I must conform to His will (Matthew 16:24-25; Romans 12:1-2).

   2. I must humble myself (Luke 14:11; Matthew 18:4).

   3. I must seek first the Kingdom of God (Matthew 6:33).

The Biblical Teaching Concerning JESUS CHRIST, PART I

Romans 1:3-4 "Concerning His Son Jesus Christ our Lord, who was born of the seed of David according to the flesh, and declared to be the Son of God with power according to the Spirit of holiness, by the resurrection from the dead."

LESSON FOURTEEN

I. What do we mean when we say that Jesus Christ has two natures?

   A. Jesus Christ is __TRUE GOD__ (Hebrews 1:8; John 20:28; Titus 2:13; I John 5:20).

      1. He is given the names and titles of __GOD__.

         a. Alpha and Omega (Revelation 22:12-13,16; 1:8).

         b. Beginning and Ending (Revelation 22:12-13,16).

         c. The Holy One (Acts 3:14 with Hosea 11:9).

66 WHAT THE BIBLE ACTUALLY TEACHES

- d. The Lord (Malachi 3:1; Luke 2:11; Acts 9:17; John 20:28; Hebrews 1:10).

- e. The Lord of Glory (I Corinthians 2:8 with Psalm 24:8-10).

- f. Wonderful, Mighty God, Father of Eternity (Isaiah 9:6).

- g. God (Hebrews 1:8; John 20:28; Titus 2:13; Romans 9:5).

- h. Immanuel (Matthew 1:23).

2. He referred to Himself as the Son of _God_ (John 5:18; Luke 22:70).

3. He has the attributes of _God_.

- a. He is all powerful (Matthew 28:18; John 5:25; Ephesians 1:20-23; Hebrews 1:3; 2:8).

- b. He is all knowing (John 2:24-25; 16:30; Colossians 2:3; Hebrews 4:12-13; Revelation 2:23).

- c. He is everywhere present (Matthew 18:20; 28:20).

- d. He is eternal (John 1:1; 17:5; 8:58; Micah 5:2).

e. He is unchanging (Hebrews 1:10-12; 13:8).

   f. He is self-existent (John 1:4; 5:21,26; Hebrews 7:16).

   g. He is holy (Acts 3:14; Mark 1:24).

4. He is an equal in the _GODHEAD_. (Philippians 2:6; II Corinthians 13:14; John 10:30-33; II Thessalonians 2:16-17; Hebrews 1:3; Colossians 1:19; 2:9).

5. He is to be worshipped as _God_. (Matthew 14:33; 28:9; Luke 24:52; Hebrews 1:6; Philippians 2:10-11; Acts 10:25-26).

B. Jesus Christ is _TRUE MAN_. (I Timothy 2:5; John 8:40).

   1. He is called the Son of _Man_ about 77 times in the New Testament (Luke 9: 22,26,44,58; 19:10).

   2. He was born of a _Woman_ (Galatians 4:4; Matthew 1:18; 2:11; 12:47; 13:55; Luke 2:7; Romans 1:3).

   3. He took on _Human_ nature (John 1:14; Hebrews 2:14; I John 4:2-3).

- a. He had a human body after His resurrection (Luke 24:39; John 20:27).

- b. He still has a human body (Acts 7:55-56; Hebrews 4:14; Acts 17:31).

4. He was subject to normal laws of _HUMAN_ development (Luke 2:40,52).

5. He was subject to physical _LIMITATIONS_ (Hebrews 4:15).

- a. He grew weary (John 4:6).

- b. He slept (Matthew 8:24).

- c. He hungered (Matthew 21:18).

- d. He thirsted (John 19:28).

- e. He wept (John 11:35).

6. He was tempted as a _MAN_ (Hebrews 2:18; 4:15).

The Biblical Teaching Concerning JESUS CHRIST, PART II

John 1:14 "And the Word became flesh and dwelt among us, and we beheld His glory, the glory as of the only begotten of the Father, full of grace and truth."

LESSON FIFTEEN

I. **Why was it necessary for the Word to become flesh?**

    A. Man is a sinner and as such is under the death penalty (Romans 3:23; 5:12; Ephesians 2:1; 4:18).

    B. God's desire is for man to be restored to life (John 10:10; I Timothy 2:4).

    C. In order for this to happen man must be redeemed and restored.

    D. No man of Adam's race can redeem men because all are in the same condition (Psalm 49:6-8).

    E. God cannot overlook man's sinfulness for He is holy.

WHAT THE BIBLE ACTUALLY TEACHES

- F. If man is to be redeemed, a sinless man must die (or pay the wages) for a sinful man.

    1. God could not redeem man as God.

    2. Angels could not redeem man because they are not of like substance.

    3. The Redeemer must be a near kinsman.

- G. If man is to be redeemed, God Himself must become man (Matthew 1:18).

III. How does Jesus Christ fulfill the qualifications for a Redeemer?

- A. He was born of _ADAM'S_ race (Matthew 1:1); hence, He is a kinsman.

- B. He did not _INHERIT_ the sin in the human bloodstream because God was His Father (I John 3:5).

- C. He was perfectly _SINLESS_ in His life; hence, He was able to redeem (I Peter 2:21-22; II Corinthians 5:21; John 14:30; 18:38).

- D. He was _WILLING_ to redeem man (Ephesians 5:25).

IV. Why did Jesus Christ have to die?

A. In order to pay the wages of sin that we had earned (I Peter 2:24; Galatians 3:10,13; Ezekiel 18:4; Romans 3:23; Genesis 2:17).

B. In order for the New Covenant to take effect (Hebrews 9:15-22).

C. In order that we might receive the adoption of sons (Galatians 4:4-5).

D. In order that He might deliver us from this present world system (Galatians 1:4).

E. In order that He might bring us to God (I Peter 3:18).

The Biblical Teaching Concerning JESUS CHRIST, PART III

Romans 5:8-9 "But God demonstrates His own love toward us, in that while we were still sinners, Christ died for us. Much more then, having now been justified by His blood, we shall be saved from wrath through Him."

LESSON SIXTEEN

V. **What was the death of Christ for man?**

   A. It was a RANSOM (Leviticus 25:47-49; Matthew 20:28; I Timothy 2:6; Galatians 3:13). A ransom means "to deliver a thing or person by paying a price; _To Buy Back_ a person or thing by paying the price for which it is held in captivity."(*The Great Doctrines of the Bible* by Evans). See Romans 7:14.

   B. It was a PROPITIATION (Romans 3:25; I John 2:2; Hebrews 2:17; 9:5).
   Propitiation means "mercy seat or covering." "The mercy seat covering of the ark of the covenant was called a propitiation. It is that by which God _Covers_, overlooks, and pardons the penitent and believing sinner because of Christ's death (Evans)."

WHAT THE BIBLE ACTUALLY TEACHES

C. It was a RECONCILIATION (Romans 5:10; II Corinthians 5:18-19; Ephesians 2:16; Colossians 1:20).
Reconciliation means <u>A BRINGING TOGETHER</u> of those who were opposed to each other. Through the cross of Christ, the enmity that existed between God and man is removed, man is brought back into fellowship with God and man's friendship with God is restored.

D. It was a SUBSTITUTION (Isaiah 53:6; I Peter 2:24; 3:18; II Corinthians 5:21; Romans 5:8; Galatians 2:20).
Substitution means "<u>IN THE PLACE OF</u> or in the stead of another." Christ was our substitute who took our place, who bore our sins, who paid the penalty that we deserved. It means that something happened to Christ "and because it happened to Christ, it need not happen to us (Evans)."

E. It was an ATONEMENT (John 1:29; I John 1:5-7).
To atone means "to cover or <u>TO MAKE AT ONE</u>."
"God foreshadowed it in the Old Testament with animal sacrifice, whose blood temporarily covered sin and the sinner, until the blood of Jesus Christ, which cleanses the sinner from all sin, was shed" (Conner).

VI. What are the benefits of the atonement?
(The following is taken from unpublished notes by Kevin J. Conner.)

A. **Pardon:** To pardon means to receive forgiveness or remission of a penalty. The penalty was paid by Jesus (Acts 10:43; 13:38-39).

B. **Justification:** In justification man is pronounced just and declared righteous. It is "just-as-if-I'd" never sinned (Romans 3:24-26; 5:1).

C. **Regeneration:** In regeneration man is born anew, experiencing a spiritual birth into the kingdom and family of God, receiving a new nature (John 3:1-5).

D. **Adoption:** In adoption the believer is placed as a child in the family of God (John 1:12; Romans 8:15; Galatians 4:5).

E. **Sanctification:** In sanctification the believer is set apart unto the Lord. He is separated **from** the world, the flesh and the devil and separated **unto** a life of serving the Lord Jesus Christ who, through His death and resurrection, brings to the believer all the benefits of the Atonement (I Corinthians 1:30; I Thessalonians 4:3; I Peter 1:2).

F. **Healing:** Whatever was lost in the fall was restored in God's atonement. It is a complete victory over all the works of darkness (Matthew 8:17; Isaiah 53:5; I Peter 2:24).

The Biblical Teaching Concerning
JESUS CHRIST, PART IV

Hebrews 7:24-25 "But He, because He continues forever, has an unchangeable priesthood. Therefore He is also able to save to the uttermost those who come to God through Him, since He always lives to make intercession for them."

LESSON SEVENTEEN

VII. What happened to Christ after His death?

    A. Christ rose from the dead (II Timothy 2:8; I Corinthians 15:4).

        1. Christ's resurrection was a physical or bodily resurrection (John 20:27; Acts 10:40-41; Luke 24:39).

        2. Christ's resurrection is one of the most important events relative to our redemption.

            a. It is referred to directly about 104 times in the New Testament.

            b. It is foundational to our justification (I Corinthians 15:14,17; Romans 4:24-25).

3. Christ's resurrection is an essential element in our confession (Romans 10:9-10).

4. Christ's resurrection is a basis for hope in our own resurrection (I Peter 1:3-4; Ephesians 1:18-20).

5. Christ's resurrection proved Him to be the Son of God (Romans 1:4).

6. Christ's resurrection fulfilled the promises to the fathers (Acts 13:32-33; 3:25-26).

B. Christ ascended to the right hand of God (Acts 1:9; 2:33-34; Hebrews 10:12).

1. Christ has been exalted by God (Philippians 2:9; Ephesians 1:20-21; Acts 5:31).

2. Christ sat down at the right hand of God (Ephesians 1:20; Colossians 3:1).

3. Christ was crowned with glory and honor (Hebrews 2:9; Ephesians 1:22; I Peter 1:21; 3:22).

VIII. What is Christ doing now?

A. Christ is involved in priestly ministry in our behalf (Hebrews 9:24).

Jesus Christ, Part IV 79

B. Christ is waiting until all enemies are put under His feet (Hebrews 10:12-13 Acts 2:34-35; 3:19-21).

C. Christ is upholding all things by the Word of His power (Hebrews 1:3-4).

IX. What does the Bible teach concerning Christ's coming again?

A. Christ is _Coming Again._
(John 14:3; Hebrews 9:28; Philippians 3:20-21; I Thessalonians 4:16-17; Acts 3:19-20).

B. Christ is coming as _Personally_, as visibly, and as gloriously as He went (Acts 1:11; I Thessalonians 4:15-17; Revelation 19; Matthew 25:31-32).

C. Christ's coming is to _Bring Hope._ to the saints (Titus 2:13; II Peter 3:11,13).

D. Christ's coming is to bring an attitude of _Watchfulness._ to all (I John 2:28; Matthew 24:44-46; Luke 12:35-36; 21:34-35).

E. Christ's coming will be _Obvious._ to all (Revelation 1:7; Matthew 24:26-27).

F. Christ's coming will take many by _Surprise._ (I Thessalonians 5:2-6; Revelation 16:15).

The Biblical Teaching Concerning ANGELS, PART I

Psalm 148:2,5 "Praise Him, all His angels; Praise Him, all His hosts! Let them praise the name of the Lord, for He commanded and they were created."

LESSON EIGHTEEN

I. **What is an angel?**

   A. Generally speaking, an angel can be an "ambassador, messenger, deputy or minister."

   1. The term is used of human messengers (Luke 7:24a).

   2. The term is used of the prophets (Haggai 1:13; Luke 7:27).

   3. The term is used of satanic messengers (II Corinthians 12:7).

   B. Specifically speaking, an angel is a finite, spiritual and celestial being (Matthew 22:30; Hebrews 1:4-7).

II. **How do we know that angels exist?**

   A. In every section of the Old Testament the existence of angels is affirmed.

WHAT THE BIBLE ACTUALLY TEACHES

      1. In the **law** (Genesis 28:12).

      2. In the **history** (II Samuel 14:20; 19:27).

      3. In the **poetry** (Psalm 34:7; 91:11; 103:20).

      4. In the **prophets** (Daniel 3:28; 6:22).

  B. In every section of the New Testament the existence of angels is affirmed.

      1. In the teaching of **Jesus** (Matthew 18:10; 13:41).

      2. In the teaching of the **Book of Acts** (Acts 5:19; 8:26; 10:1-7).

      3. In the teaching of **Paul** and the other **Apostles** (II Thessalonians 1:7; I Peter 3:22; Jude 9).

III. Why is the existence of angels questioned by some?
(The following is taken from unpublished notes by Kevin J. Conner.)

  A. __UNBELIEF__ in the supernatural (Acts 23:8).

  B. __IGNORANCE__ of what the Scripture teaches.

C. _FEAR._ of the unseen or invisible realm of spirit beings.

D. _UNDUE ADORATION_ and the worship of angels, which is forbidden by the Word of God (Colossians 2:18; Revelation 22:8-9).

IV. **What names and titles are ascribed to angels in the Bible?**

   A. Minister or Servant (Psalm 104:4).

   B. Host or Army (Luke 2:13).

   C. Watchers (Daniel 4:13,17).

   D. Sons of the Mighty or Mighty Ones (Psalm 89:6; 29:1).

   E. Sons of God (Job 1:6; 2:1; 38:7).

   F. Holy Ones (Psalm 89:6-7; Daniel 4:13).

   G. Morning Stars (Job 38:7).

   H. Ministering Spirits (Hebrews 1:13-14).

   I. Flames of Fire (Hebrews 1:7).

V. **What is the nature of angels?**

A. Angels are _CREATED BEINGS._
 (Colossians 1:16; Psalm 148:2,5).

   1. They are each individually created for they do not reproduce after their kind (Matthew 22:28-30).

   2. They are each individually created and therefore referred to as "sons of God" (Job 1:6; 2:1).

   3. They are each individually created and hence they are dependent, finite, and limited.

   4. They were created prior to the creation of the earth (Job 38:4-7).

B. Angels are _SPIRITUAL BEINGS._
 (Hebrews 1:14; Psalm 104:4).

   1. Angels are not limited by natural bodies, yet at times they appeared to men in visible, even human form (Genesis 19; Judges 2:1; 6:11-12).

   2. Angels are limited by space even though they are spiritual (Daniel 9:21-23; 10:10-14).

C. Angels are _IMMORTAL._
 (Luke 20:36); therefore, once they are created, they never cease to exist.

Angels, Part I

D. Angels have all the elements of _PERSONALITY_.

1. They have intellect (Matthew 28:5; I Peter 1:12).

   a. In intellect they are superior to man (II Samuel 14:17).

   b. In intellect they are inferior to God (Matthew 24:36; I Peter 1:12).

2. They have emotions (Job 38:7; Luke 15:10).

3. They have a will (Isaiah 14:12-15; II Peter 2:4; Jude 6).

The Biblical Teaching Concerning ANGELS, PART II

Hebrews 1:13-14 "But to which of the angels has He ever said: 'Sit at My right hand, till I make Your enemies Your footstool'? Are they not all ministering spirits sent forth to minister for those who will inherit salvation?"

LESSON NINETEEN

VI. **What are some other things that we know about angels?**

A. Angels are mighty, having _GREAT POWER_.
(Psalm 103:20; II Kings 19:35; Isaiah 37:36).

1. Their power is greater than man (II Peter 2:11).

2. Their power is delegated to them (II Thessalonians 1:7).

B. Angels exist in various _RANKS_ and orders.

1. There are Seraphim (Isaiah 6:2-6).

2. There are Cherubim (Genesis 3:24; Ezekiel 10).

WHAT THE BIBLE ACTUALLY TEACHES

3. There are Archangels (Jude 9; I Thessalonians 4:16).

4. There was the Angel of the Lord (Judges 13; Exodus 3:2-15; Genesis 32:24-32).

C. Angels are very many in _NUMBER_. (Hebrews 12:22; Matthew 26:53; Daniel 7:10; Psalm 68:17).

D. Angels are _GLORIOUS_ beings (Luke 9:26).

E. Angels dwell in _HEAVENLY PLACES_. (Matthew 22:30; Ephesians 3:10; John 1:51).

VII. What is the ministry and function of the angels?

A. Angels have a primary _MINISTRY UNTO GOD_.

1. They were created to bring glory to God (Colossians 1:16; Revelation 4:6-11; Psalm 148:2).

2. They are ministers of worship unto God (Isaiah 6:3; Revelation 5:8-13).

3. They have a type of priestly ministry in the heavenly sanctuary (Hebrews 1:7).

4. They execute the will of God (Psalm 103:20).

a. In controlling nature (Revelation 7:1).

b. In governing nations (Daniel 10:13,21; 12:1).

c. In executing God's judgments (Genesis 19:1; Psalm 78:43,49).

B. Angels have a unique _MINISTRY TO GOD'S PEOPLE._

1. They protect the people of God (Psalm 35:4-5; 34:7; II Kings 6:13-17; Isaiah 63:9; Daniel 12:1; Hebrews 1:14).

2. They guide the believer at times (Acts 8:26; 10:3).

3. They minister to the physical needs of God's people (I Kings 19:7).

4. They strengthen and encourage the believer (Matthew 4:11; Luke 22:43; Acts 5:19-20; 27:24).

5. They seem to have a special ministry to children (Matthew 18:10).

6. They serve as agents in the answering of our prayers (Daniel 10:10-12; Acts 12:1-17).

7. They carry those who die in the Lord home (Luke 16:22).

8. They will come with Christ for the believers at the Second Coming (II Thessalonians 1:7-8; Matthew 25:31-32).

VIII. What specific area of God's dealing with man has <u>not</u> been entrusted to angels?

Angels do not preach the Gospel. This task has been assigned to man (I Peter 1:12; Acts 10; 11:13-14).

The Biblical Teaching Concerning
THE HOLY SPIRIT, PART I

John 15:26 "But when the Helper comes, whom I shall send to you from the Father, the Spirit of truth who proceeds from the Father, He will testify of Me."

LESSON TWENTY

I. Is the Holy Spirit part of the Godhead?

YES! The Holy Spirit is God for the following reasons:

A. The Holy Spirit is described as having the same <u>ATTRIBUTES AS GOD</u>.

1. Eternal (Hebrews 9:14).

2. Omnipresent (Psalm 139:7-10).

3. Omnipotent (Luke 1:35; Romans 15:13).

4. Omniscient (I Corinthians 2:10-11; John 14:26).

5. Love (Romans 15:30).

6. Holiness (Romans 1:4).

WHAT THE BIBLE ACTUALLY TEACHES

B. The Holy Spirit does the __WORKS OF GOD__.

1. Creation (Job 33:4; Psalm 104:30).

2. Inspiration of prophecy and scripture (II Peter 1:21; II Samuel 23:2-3).

3. Regeneration (John 3:5-8).

4. Conviction (John 16:8).

5. Comforting (John 14:16).

6. Intercession (Romans 8:26).

7. Sanctification (II Thessalonians 2:13).

8. Giving divine gifts (I Corinthians 12:4-11).

9. Begetting Christ (Luke 1:35).

10. Empowering the believer (Acts 1:8).

C. The name of the Holy Spirit is coupled with the Father and the Son (Matthew 28:19; Acts 2:38-39; II Corinthians 13:14; I John 5:7-8; Hebrews 9:14; Ephesians 2:18; I Corinthians 12:4-6).

D. The Holy Spirit is called __GOD__ (Acts 5:3-4; II Corinthians 3:18 NAS).

The Holy Spirit, Part I

II. Is the Holy Spirit a person or merely a heavenly influence?

The Holy Spirit is a person for the following reasons:

A. Jesus referred to the Holy Spirit as __A PERSON.__ (John 14:16-17; 15:26; 16:7-8,13-14).

B. The Holy Spirit has the three elements of personality.

1. A mind (Romans 8:27).

2. A will (I Corinthians 12:11).

3. Emotions (Romans 8:26-27; 15:30).

C. The Holy Spirit performs __ACTIONS__ that only a person can perform.

1. He speaks (I Timothy 4:1; Revelation 2:7,11,17,29).

2. He searches all things (I Corinthians 2:10).

3. He reveals or inspires (II Peter 1:21).

4. He teaches (John 14:26).

5. He cries (Galatians 4:6).

WHAT THE BIBLE ACTUALLY TEACHES

6. He intercedes (Romans 8:26).

7. He calls and places men in service (Acts 13:2; 20:28).

8. He leads (Romans 8:14; Matthew 4:1).

9. He rules (Act 16:6-7).

10. He creates (Job 33:4).

11. He sanctifies (Romans 15:16).

12. He helps (Romans 8:26).

13. He gives gifts (I Corinthians 12:7-11).

14. He works miracles (Acts 2:4; 8:39).

15. He bears witness (I John 5:6).

16. He reproves (John 16:8-11).

17. He regenerates (John 3:5-6).

18. He strives with men (Genesis 6:3).

19. He guides into truth (John 16:13).

20. He sends (Isaiah 48:16).

D. The Holy Spirit has *PERSONAL FEELINGS* ascribed to Him.

1. He can be grieved (Ephesians 4:30).

2. He can be vexed or rebelled against (Isaiah 63:10).

3. He can be insulted (Hebrews 10:29).

4. He can be lied to (Acts 5:3).

5. He can be blasphemed (Matthew 12:31-32).

6. He can be resisted (Acts 7:51).

7. He can be put to the test (Acts 5:9).

8. He can be quenched (I Thessalonians 5:19).

9. He can be provoked (Psalm 106:33).

10. He can be pleased (Acts 15:28).

III. How important is the Holy Spirit in our lives?

In many ways the Holy Spirit should be the closest relationship that we have.

A. The Holy Spirit is the one who __DRAWS__ the unbeliever to God (I Corinthians 12:3).

B. The Holy Spirit is the __ADMINISTRATOR__ of the promises of God (John 16:14-15).

WHAT THE BIBLE ACTUALLY TEACHES

    C. The Holy Spirit is the one who _DWELLS_ within the spirit of the believer (I Corinthians 6:19).

    D. The Holy Spirit is the one who _EMPOWERS_ us for service (Acts 1:8).

    E. The Holy Spirit is the one who _ANOINTS_ our ministry (Acts 10:38; I John 2:27).

    F. The Holy Spirit is the one who _SANCTIFIES_ us (Romans 15:16).

The Biblical Teaching Concerning
THE HOLY SPIRIT, PART II

Isaiah 11:2 "The Spirit of the Lord shall rest upon Him, the Spirit of wisdom and understanding, the Spirit of counsel and might, the Spirit of knowledge and of the fear of the Lord."

LESSON TWENTY ONE

IV. **What are some of the names and titles ascribed to the Holy Spirit?**

   A. Names and titles tell us a great deal about a person, his nature and his work.

   B. There are about fifty names and titles given to the Holy Spirit in the Bible and all of them emphasize some unique aspect of the work and ministry of the Holy Spirit. Some of these include:

   1. The Spirit of God (I Corinthians 3:16).

   2. The Holy Spirit (Luke 11:13) or the Spirit of Holiness (Romans 1:4).

   3. The Spirit of your Father (Matthew 10:20).

WHAT THE BIBLE ACTUALLY TEACHES

    4. The Spirit of Him who raised Jesus from the dead (Romans 1:4; 8:11; I Peter 3:18).

    5. The Power of the Highest (Luke 1:35).

    6. The Breath of the Almighty (Job 33:4; 32:8).

    7. The Spirit of Grace (Hebrews 10:29).

    8. The Comforter (John 14:16).

    9. The Spirit of Truth (John 14:17).

    10. The Spirit of Life (Romans 8:2).

    11. The Spirit of Adoption (Romans 8:15).

    12. The Spirit of Promise (Ephesians 1:13-14).

    13. The Spirit of Love (II Timothy 1:17).

    14. The Finger of God (Luke 11:20).

V. What are some of the most common symbols that are applied to the Holy Spirit?

    A. The Dove (Luke 3:22).

        1. The dove is symbolic of _Purity_ (Matthew 10:16).

The Holy Spirit, Part II 99

2. The dove is symbolic of _Gentleness_ (Galatians 5:22-23).

3. The dove is symbolic of _Constancy in Love._ (Song of Solomon 5:12).

B. Fire (Revelation 4:5; Isaiah 4:4).

1. Fire purifies (Isaiah 6:7).

2. Fire tests (I Corinthians 3:13-15).

3. Fire illuminates (Psalm 78:14; Ephesians 1:17-18).

C. Oil (I John 2:20,27).

1. Oil is associated with anointing for service (Acts 10:38).

2. Oil is associated with healing (Psalm 23:5; James 5:14).

3. Oil is associated with consecration and dedication (Genesis 28:18; Leviticus 8:30).

D. Water (Exodus 17:6 with I Corinthians 10:1-3).

1. Water speaks of _Refreshing._ (John 4:14).

WHAT THE BIBLE ACTUALLY TEACHES

    2. Water speaks of _Cleansing_ (Hebrews 10:22).

    3. Water speaks of _Life_ (John 7:38-39).

E. Wind (John 3:8).

    1. Wind is mysterious in its work (I Corinthians 2:14; John 3:8).

    2. Wind is powerful in its action (Acts 2:2-3).

    3. Wind or breath is necessary for life (John 3:6-8; Ezekiel 37:7-10).

F. Other symbols of the Holy Spirit include:

    1. The Seal (Ephesians 1:13).

    2. The Earnest (Ephesians 1:14).

    3. The Rain (Acts 2:17-18).

    4. Wine (Acts 2:13-15; Ephesians 5:18).

The Biblical Teaching Concerning THE HOLY SPIRIT, PART III

John 16:8-11 "And when He has come, He will convict the world of sin, and of righteousness, and of judgment: of sin, because they do not believe in Me; of righteousness, because I go to My Father and you see Me no more; of judgment, because the ruler of this world is judged."

LESSON TWENTY TWO

VI. What is the work and ministry of the Holy Spirit?

    A. The Holy Spirit was at work in relation to Christ who patterns for us that which the Church as the Body of Christ is to experience. Christ was:

        1. Born of the Spirit (Luke 1:35; John 3:5).

        2. Baptized with the Spirit (Matthew 3:16-17; Acts 1:4-5).

        3. Filled with the Spirit (Luke 4:1; Ephesians 3:19).

        4. Led of the Spirit (Matthew 4:1; Romans 8:14).

5. Empowered by the Spirit (Luke 4:14; Acts 1:8).

6. Anointed by the Spirit (Acts 10:38; I John 2:27).

7. Ministering by the Spirit (Luke 4:18; I Peter 1:11-12).

8. Sealed by the Spirit (John 6:27; II Corinthians 1:21-22).

9. Raised from the dead by the Spirit (Romans 8:11; 8:2,13).

10. Giving commandments by the Spirit (Acts 1:2; 15:28-29).

B. The Holy Spirit has an important work in the life of every believer.

1. He convicts the unbeliever of sin (John 16:8-11; Isaiah 40:7).

2. He indwells the spirit of the believer (Romans 8:9; I Corinthians 6:17).

3. He gives assurance of salvation (Romans 8:16; Galatians 4:6).

4. He empowers the believer to fulfill the commands of Christ (Acts 1:8).

The Holy Spirit, Part III 103

5. He opens the believer's understanding to the things of God (I Corinthians 2:12).

6. He renews the believer (Titus 3:5).

7. He produces Christ-like fruit in the life of the believer (Galatians 5:22-23).

8. He teaches the believer and leads him into truth (John 16:13).

9. He strengthens the believer in the inner man (Ephesians 3:16).

10. He inspires the believer to worship (Philippians 3:3).

11. He calls the believer into service (Acts 13:2-4).

12. He guides the believers in their ministry (Acts 8:29; 16:6-7).

13. He imparts spiritual gifts to the believer (I Corinthians 2:7-11).

14. He assists the believer in times of persecution (Matthew 10:19-20).

15. He comforts and gives encouragement to the believer (John 15:26; Acts 9:31).

16. He preserves the believer in this world (I Peter 1:5).

17. He assists the believer in prayer (Romans 8:26-28).

18. He transforms the believer into the image of Christ (II Corinthians 3:18).

VII. Why is it so important to know the Holy Spirit?

A. Because a lack of intimate knowledge and relationship of the Holy Spirit can keep us out of much of the _BLESSING OF GOD._ (Acts 19:1-6).

B. Because we are living in a day when _A SPECIAL OUTPOURING_ of the Holy Spirit has been promised (Acts 2:17-21; Joel 2:28-32; James 5:7-8).

C. Because the Holy Spirit is the _FINAL PERSON_ of the Godhead to witness and call us before the culmination of time (I John 5:6-13; Matthew 12:31-32; Revelation 22:17).

The Biblical Teaching Concerning
THE CHURCH, PART I

Matthew 16:18-19 "And I also say to you that you are Peter, and on this rock I will build My church, and the gates of Hades shall not prevail against it. And I will give you the keys of the kingdom of heaven, and whatever you bind on earth will be bound in heaven, and whatever you loose on earth will be loosed in heaven."

LESSON TWENTY THREE

I. **Why is it so important to study the doctrine of the Church?**

   A. Because the Church is the _Only Institution_ that Christ ever purposed to build (Matthew 16:18).

   B. Because the Church was in _God's Plan_ from the foundation of the world (Ephesians 1:3-5, 9-12; II Timothy 1:9).

   C. Because the Church is the _Vehicle_ through which God's eternal purposes will be accomplished (Ephesians 3:8-11).

D. Because the Church is the apple of God's eye and the ___BRIDE OF CHRIST___ (Ephesians 5:25-32).

II. What does the word "church" mean?

A. Because of the English use of the word church, we may have a wrong understanding of the biblical meaning. The church as spoken of in the Bible is not:

1. A building for Christian worship, as "we built a new church last year."

2. A regular religious service or public worship, as "we went to church on Sunday."

3. A denomination or sect, as "the Roman church, Pentecostal church or Presbyterian church, etc."

B. The word church in the New Testament comes from the Greek word *ekklesia* which literally means ___CALLED OUT ONES___.

1. In Greek society an *ekklesia* was an assembly of free citizens called out from their homes or places of business to give consideration to matters of public interest (Acts 19:32,39,41).

2. In relation to God's people, it refers to all those people who have been called out

from the world (I Peter 2:9) who have separated themselves unto God and have gathered unto the Lord for worship and fellowship.

III. What did Jesus teach concerning the Church?

Jesus specifically mentioned the church _TWICE_ in His teaching and in each case He referred to a different aspect of the church.

A. In Matthew 16:13-19 Jesus referred to the _UNIVERSAL CHURCH_ (also called the invisible church) that consists of all believers living and dead from all ages who have been called out of the world system and who have separated themselves unto Christ.

Jesus implied that the universal church would be:

1. Based on the confession of Jesus Christ as the Son of God (vs 15-17).

2. Built by Christ Himself when He said "I will build" (vs 18).

3. Owned by Christ Himself when He said "**My** church" (vs 18).

4. Unified into one when He said "church" not "churches" (vs 18).

WHAT THE BIBLE ACTUALLY TEACHES

5. Victorious over the powers of hell (vs 18-19).

6. Powerfully administrating God's heavenly kingdom on earth (vs 19).

7. Fully supported by heaven's authority (vs 19).

(Note: Other references to the invisible church include Ephesians 1:22; 3:10; 3:21; 5:25-32).

B. In Matthew 18:15-20 Jesus referred to the <u>LOCAL CHURCH</u>. (also called the visible church) or as a specific body of believers in a given locality.

Jesus implied that the local church would be:

1. Composed of people who are called brothers (vs 15).

2. An assembly where accountability exists between members (vs 15-17).

3. An assembly where discipline occurs (vs 15-17).

4. An assembly where God has established authority (vs 18).

5. A defined body from which you could be expelled (vs 17).

6. An assembly of fellowship in faith and prayer (vs 19).

7. An assembly where Christ promises to dwell in the midst (vs 20).

8. An assembly that gathers around the name of Christ (vs 20).

9. An assembly that bears the authority of heaven (vs 18).

10. An assembly whose success is going to be dependent upon a lot of love, patience and forgiveness.

IV. What aspect of the Church becomes the major focus of the New Testament?

A. Out of approximately 110 references to the Church of Jesus Christ in the New Testament, clearly 96 of these references refer to the _LOCAL OR THE VISIBLE CHURCH._

B. As believers, it is vital that we focus on and emphasize what God emphasizes.

The Biblical Teaching Concerning THE CHURCH, PART II

Hebrews 12:22-24 "But you have come to Mount Zion and to the city of the living God, the heavenly Jerusalem, to an innumerable company of angels, to the general assembly and church of the firstborn who are registered in heaven, to God the Judge of all, to the spirits of just men made perfect, to Jesus the Mediator of the new covenant, and to the blood of sprinkling that speaks better things than that of Abel."

LESSON TWENTY FOUR

V. What are some of the names and titles of the church?

    A. There are many names and titles associated with the church. Each one of these refer to a different aspect of the church which is God's manifold wisdom (Ephesians 3:9-10).

        1. The City of the Living God (Hebrews 12:22).

        2. The Church of the Firstborn (Hebrews 12:23).

        3. The House of the Lord (Hebrews 3:6; I Timothy 3:15).

4. The Church of the Living God (I Timothy 3:15).

5. The Pillar and Ground of Truth (I Timothy 3:15).

6. The Israel of God (Galatians 6:16).

7. Mount Zion (Hebrews 12:22).

8. Heavenly Jerusalem (Galatians 4:26; Hebrews 12:22).

9. God's Husbandry or Field (I Corinthians 3:9).

10. A Golden Lampstand (Revelation 1:20).

B. Actually there are over seventy names and titles in both the Old and New Testaments that refer directly or indirectly to the Church of Jesus Christ.

VI. **What is the relationship of the Church in the Old Testament and the Church in the New Testament?**

A. In the Old Testament God had His "called out ones." Israel was God's chosen nation who was to be His instrument to touch the nations and bring forth the Messiah (Acts 7:38).

1. Israel was an object of God's grace (Deuteronomy 7:6-10).

2. Israel was called out of bondage (Exodus 3:7-8).

3. Israel experienced a passover deliverance (Exodus 12).

4. Israel became separated unto God by virtue of baptism in the sea and in the cloud (I Corinthians 10:1-4).

5. Israel was to be distinct from the pagan nations (Exodus 11:7; Leviticus 20:22-26).

B. In the New Testament God has His "called out ones." The Church is God's chosen nation which has become His instrument to touch the nations and demonstrate kingdom glories and virtues (I Peter 2:4-10).

1. We were objects of God's _GRACE_. (Ephesians 2:8-9).

2. We were called out _OF BONDAGE_. (Ephesians 2:1-3).

3. We have experienced our _PASSOVER_ deliverance (I Corinthians 5:7-8).

4. We have been _SEPERATED_ unto God by virtue of water baptism and spirit baptism (Acts 2:38-39; Romans 6-8).

5. We are to be distinct from the _WORLD SYSTEM_. (John 15:18-19; 17:14-17; II Corinthians 6:14-18).

C. There is a connection between the church of the Old Testament and the church of the New Testament.

1. The Old Testament church, which was established by the prophets, serves as a foundation for the New Testament church established by the apostles (Ephesians 2:19-22).

2. The Old Testament church looked forward to Christ while the New Testament church is built upon Christ (I Peter 2:6-8; I Corinthians 3:10-11).

3. The connection is seen in the titles given to the people of God in both the Old and New Testaments.

Title	O.T. Church	N.T. Church
A Chosen People	Dt 10:15	I Pe 2:9
A Holy Nation	Ex 19:6	I Pe 2:9
A Priesthood	Ex 19:6	I Pe 2:9
The People of God	Ps 100:3	II Co 6:16
Israel	Isa 44:6	Gal 6:16
The Flock of God	Jer 23:3	I Pe 5:2
A Light	Isa 60:1,3	Mt 5:14
God's Witness	Isa 43:10	Ac 1:8

4. The great mystery hidden for ages but preached by the apostles was that the Jew and the Gentiles were made one (Ephesians 2:14; 3:5-6), in one body, one building, built upon the foundation laid by the Old Testament prophets and the New Testament apostles, Christ being the Chief Cornerstone (Ephesians 2:20-22).

The Biblical Teaching Concerning
THE CHURCH, PART III

Ephesians 2:19-22 "Now, therefore, you are no longer strangers and foreigners, but fellow citizens with the saints and members of the household of God, having been built on the foundation of the apostles and prophets, Jesus Christ Himself being the chief cornerstone, in whom the whole building being joined together, grows into a holy temple in the Lord, in whom you also are being built together for a habitation of God in the Spirit."

LESSON TWENTY FIVE

VII. What does the book of Ephesians reveal to us about the Church?

> The book of Ephesians has been titled "The Book of the Church" because of the rich revelation concerning the church found in it. Five beautiful pictures of the church are found in Ephesians, each one filling out and adding to our overall understanding of and appreciation for the church.

A. The Church as the _TEMPLE OF GOD_ (Ephesians 2:19-22).

1. A temple (i.e. the church) is to be a habitation for God (Ephesians 2:22).

2. A temple is built by someone (Hebrews 3:1-6).

3. A temple is composed of stones (I Peter 2:4).

4. A temple is a place where a priesthood functions (I Peter 2:4).

5. A temple is a place of sacrifice (I Peter 2:4).

B. The Church as the _FAMILY OF GOD._ (Ephesians 3:14-15).

1. In the family we have a heavenly Father (Galatians 4:4-7).

2. In the family we have a firstborn, elder brother (Hebrews 2:14-17).

3. In the family we have other brothers and sisters (I Peter 1:22).

4. In the family we are all partakers of the same blood (Ephesians 2:13).

5. In the family we all share in the same name (Revelation 22:4).

6. In the family we share a common inheritance (I Peter 1:3-4).

C. The Church as the __Body of Christ__ (Ephesians 4:7-16).

1. Each member of the body has a unique function (Romans 12:4-5).

2. Each member of the body is inter-related to other members (I Corinthians 12:17).

3. Each member of the body submits to the one head (Ephesians 1:22-27).

4. Each member of the body is vital and necessary (I Corinthians 12:19-26).

D. The Church as the __Bride of Christ__ (Ephesians 5:25-32).

1. As the bride we are espoused to one husband (II Corinthians 11:2).

2. As the bride we must make ourselves ready (Revelation 19:7-8).

3. As the bride we must enter into covenantal relationship with Christ (I Corinthians 6:16-17).

4. As the bride we must remain faithful and keep ourselves pure (II Corinthians 11:2).

5. As the bride we will be part of a great wedding celebration (Revelation 19:6-10).

E. The Church as the __ARMY OF GOD__ (Ephesians 6:10-20).

    1. In the army we have a captain and a chief leader (Hebrews 2:10).

    2. In the army we are enlisted as good soldiers (II Timothy 2:3-4).

    3. In the army we are involved in spiritual warfare (Ephesians 6:12).

    4. In the army the armor is provided by God (Ephesians 6:13-18).

    5. In the army our weapons are not carnal but mighty (II Corinthians 10:3-5).

    6. In the army of God we will be victorious and be instrumental in destroying the gates of hell (Matthew 16:18).

VIII. **What is the ministry and mission of the Church?**

The church has a four-fold ministry.

A. The church has a ministry to __THE LORD__. The chief ministry of the church is that of worshipping and glorifying God (I Corinthians 10:31).

The Church, Part III

B. The church has a ministry to _ITSELF_. The members of the church have a responsibility to do everything they can to build or edify the church (Ephesians 4:9-16; I Corinthians 14:12).

C. The church has a ministry to _THE WORLD_ (Matthew 28:18-20; Mark 16:15-20). The church is to take the gospel to the ends of the earth and teach men and women the ways of God.

D. The church has a ministry to _PRINCIPALITIES AND POWERS_ (Ephesians 1:20-23; I Corinthians 15:24-26). The church is going to be used by God to bring about the downfall and utter demise of Satan and his evil hosts (Romans 16:20).

The Biblical Teaching Concerning
HEAVEN AND HELL

Hebrews 9:27-28 "And as it is appointed for men to die once, but after this the judgment, so Christ was offered once to bear the sins of many. To those who eagerly wait for Him He will appear the second time, apart from sin, for salvation."

LESSON TWENTY SIX

I. **What happens to people when they die?**

At death, the body of every man, woman and child goes to the grave to await a future resurrection (Genesis 3:19; Job 5:26). However, the soul (the eternal part) of man does not (II Peter 1:13-14).

    A. The soul of the believer _goes to be with Christ._ until the believer experiences the first resurrection (Revelation 20:5-6).

        1. Stephen, the church's first martyr, called upon Jesus to receive his spirit (Acts 7:59).

        2. Jesus told the repentant thief that he would be with Him that very day (Luke 23:43).

3. Paul indicates that to be absent from the body is to be present with Christ (II Corinthians 5:1-8, esp 6-8).

B. The soul of the unbeliever goes to "Hades" (New Testament word) or "Sheol" (Old Testament word), which is the _PLACE OF THE DEAD_. to await the second resurrection (Revelation 20:11-15).

II. Is there a judgement after death?

> YES! There is a judgment in relation to the believer, and there is a judgment in relation to the unbeliever.

A. The judgment of the believer follows the first resurrection and is referred to as the _JUDGMENT SEAT OF CHRIST_ (II Corinthians 5:10).

1. This judgment involves believers only and does not deal with the issue of forgiven sin and the salvation of the believer (Ephesians 2:8-10).

2. This judgment concerns the believer's faithfulness to all the will of God (Luke 12:42-48).

3. This judgment concerns the believer's works of service rendered to Christ in this life (I Corinthians 3:12-15; Matthew 16:27).

4. This judgment is followed by corresponding rewards for a life lived for Christ (I Timothy 4:8; Revelation 11:18).

5. Other related verses: Romans 14:8-12; I John 4:17; II Timothy 4:1.

B. The judgment of the unbeliever follows the second resurrection and is referred to as the <u>GREAT WHITE THRONE JUDGMENT</u> (Revelation 20:11-15).

1. This judgment involves those whose name is not written in the Book of Life (Revelation 20:15).

2. This judgment will settle all accounts and render the wages of sin and the reward of iniquity (II Peter 2:12-17; Acts 1:18).

III. What is heaven going to be like?

WHAT THE BIBLE ACTUALLY TEACHES

> Heaven is an indescribably wonderful place that was created by God for His enjoyment with His creation.

- A. It is a place of **God's Dwelling**. (II Chronicles 6:30; Revelation 21:22-24).

- B. It is a place of **Enjoyment**. (Revelation 22:1-5).

    1. No sin, sickness, disease or death (Revelation 21:4,27).

    2. No tears, pain or suffering (Revelation 21:4).

- C. It is a place of rejoicing in **God's Presence**. (Revelation 14:1-5).

- D. It is a place of enjoying **Fulfilled Promises**. (Revelation 22:5).

IV. Is there a literal hell?

Yes! Hell is a literal place that was prepared for Satan and his fallen angels but will also become an eternal place of judgment for all those who follow Satan's pernicious ways (Matthew 10:28; 18:9; 23:33; 25:41).

V. What will hell be like?

> Hell is an indescribably vile place, totally void of God's presence.

    A.   Hell is a place of __TORMENT__ (Revelation 14:9-11; Luke 16:23).

        1.   It is a place of full consciousness (Luke 16:19-31).

        2.   It is a place where the fire of desires, lusts and appetites are never quenched (Mark 9:43-48).

        3.   It is a place of wicked companions (Matthew 23:14-15,33).

        4.   It is a place of groaning, weeping and wailing (Matthew 13:42,50).

        5.   It is a place of fire and brimstone (Mark 9:43-49).

        6.   It is a place of everlasting shame and contempt (Daniel 12:2).

B. Hell is _ETERNAL_. (Daniel 12:2; Matthew 25:46; Jude 7; Revelation 20:10).

VI. **What makes our life on earth and the decisions that we make so important?**

A. Because death is final (Hebrews 9:27).

B. Because after death there are no second chances (Luke 16:19-31; Ecclesiastes 11:3; Ezekiel 18:19-32).

C. Because our eternal destiny is determined on the basis of what we do in and with this life (I Corinthians 3:10-15).

D. Because heaven and hell are eternal states (Revelation 20:10; 22:5).

WHAT THE BIBLE ACTUALLY TEACHES ANSWER KEY

Lesson 1
- I. B. All that the Bible
- III. A. Jesus
  - B. The disciples
  - C. Paul
  - D. The early church
  - E. 1. Righteous living
    - 2. Christian freedom
    - 3. Sanctification
    - 4. Maturity
    - 5. Life
  - F. By deception
- IV. A. Sound
  - B. Pure
  - C. Scripture
  - D. Practiced

Lesson 2
- II. A. Divinely inspired
  - B. The final authority
  - C. Obedience
- III. A. 1. Creation
  - 2. Conscience
  - 3. Divine intervention

Lesson 3
- IV. A. Hammer
  - B. Mirror
  - C. Two-edged sword
  - D. Judge
  - E. Water
  - F. Seed
  - G. Food
  - H. Lamp

    I. True riches
    J. Fire

Lesson 4
  V. A. Full or complete
          1. The entire Book
          2. Every area
      B. 1. The very words
          3. Without error
          Every one
      C. God-breathed
 VI. A. Of communicating
      B. To understand
      C. To write down

Lesson 5
 II. B. 1. Declares it
          2. Knowledge of God
 IV. A. Spirit
      B. Light
      C. Love
      D. Consuming Fire

Lesson 6
  V. A. 4. Everything
          5. Everything
          6. Wisdom
          7. Everywhere
      B. 1. Holy
          2. Love
          3. Faithful
          4. Righteous or just
          5. Mercy

Answer Key

Lesson 7
- VI. A. One
  - B. Plurality
  - C. Tri-unity
- VII. A. 1. God
  - 2. God
  - 3. God

Lesson 8
- I. A. 1. Inferior to God
  - 2. Finite
  - B. Angelic order
  - C. Highest rank
- III. B. Author of sin
  - C. Against God
  - D. God's purposes

Lesson 9
- V. A. Powerful
  - B. The victory
    1. Armor and weapons
    2. Intercedes
    3. Confidence
    4. Power
    5. Increase
    6. Along side us
    7. Divine tests
    8. Unity
    9. Sickness
    10. Legal Right

Lesson 10
- I. A. 1. As a three-fold being
  - a. God-conscious

            b. Self-conscious
            c. Sense-conscious
         2. As an intelligent being
         3. As a moral being
     B. As a dependent being
     C. Be inhabited
     D. Love
II. B. 1. Body
         2. Soul
         3. Spirit

Lesson 11
IV. A. Born
     B. No inclination
     C. No understanding
     D. Defiled
     E. Slave
     F. Wrath
     G. Enemy
     H. Dead
     I. Damnation

Lesson 12
I. A. 1. An accident
        2. Weaknesses of the flesh
        3. Various world calamities
        4. A necessity
        5. Excusable
II. A. Through Satan
    B. Through Adam

Lesson 13
III. A. Heavenly places
     B. Natural earth

Answer Key

        C. Animal kingdom
        D. Entire race of mankind
V. A. Self-will
    B. Pride
    C. Covetousness
    D. Unbelief

Lesson 14
I. A. True God
      1. God
      2. God
      3. God
      4. Godhead
      5. God
   B. True man
      1. Man
      2. Woman
      3. Human
      4. Human
      5. Limitations
      6. Man

Lesson 15
III. A. Adam's
     B. Inherit
     C. Sinless
     D. Willing

Lesson 16
V. A. To buy back
    B. Covers
    C. A bringing together
    D. In the place of
    E. To make at one

134 WHAT THE BIBLE ACTUALLY TEACHES

Lesson 17
- IX. A. Coming again
  - B. Personally
  - C. Bring hope
  - D. Watchfulness
  - E. Obvious
  - F. Surprise

Lesson 18
- III. A. Unbelief
  - B. Ignorance
  - C. Fear
  - D. Undue adoration
- V. A. Created beings
  - B. Spiritual beings
  - C. Immortal
  - D. Personality

Lesson 19
- VI. A. Great power
  - B. Ranks
  - C. Number
  - D. Glorious
  - E. Heavenly places
- VII. A. Ministry unto God
  - B. Ministry to God's people

Lesson 20
- I. A. Attributes as God
  - B. Works of God
  - D. God
- II. A. A person
  - C. Actions
  - D. Personal feelings

Answer Key **135**

    III. A. Draws
           B. Administrator
           C. Dwells
           D. Empowers
           E. Anoints
           F. Sanctifies

Lesson 21
    V. A. 1. Purity
               2. Gentleness
               3. Constancy in love
        D. 1. Refreshing
               2. Cleansing
               3. Life

Lesson 22
    VII. A. Blessing of God
           B. A special outpouring
           C. Final person

Lesson 23
    I. A. Only institution
        B. God's plan
        C. Vehicle
        D. Bride of Christ
    II. B. Called out ones
    III. Twice
        A. Universal church
        B. Local church
    IV. A. Local or the visible church

Lesson 24
    VI. B. 1. Grace
               2. Of bondage

3. Passover
4. Separated
5. World system

Lesson 25
VII. A. Temple of God
    B. Family of God
    C. Body of Christ
    D. Bride of Christ
    E. Army of God
VIII. A. The Lord
    B. Itself
    C. The world
    D. Principalities and powers

Lesson 26
I. A. Goes to be with Christ
   B. Place of the dead
II. A. Judgment Seat of Christ
   B. Great White Throne Judgment
III. A. God's dwelling
    B. Enjoyment
    C. God's presence
    D. Fulfilled promises
V. A. Torment
   B. Eternal